Sun and Stork

A CONTEMPORARY FOLKTALE
WRITTEN AND ILLUSTRATED BY CRYSTAL BENTLEY

THE STORY OF SUN'S INCREDIBLE GIFT!
IF YOU DON'T KNOW WHY HUMANS COME IN SUCH A BEAUTIFUL ARRAY OF COLORS, YOU WILL ONCE YOU READ THE STORY OF SUN AND STORK.

SUN AND STORK
A Contemporary Folktale

Story and illustrations Copyright 2020: Crystal Bentley
Cover and Book Layout: Edward Bentley
All rights reserved

No part of this publication may be reproduced, stored in a retrieval system or transmitted in any form or by any means—electronic, mechanical, photocopying, recording, or otherwise—without prior written permission of the publisher.

Printed in the United States of America

Self-published by Sun and Stork Publishing
www.SunAndStorkPublishing.com

ISBN: 978-1-7352279-1-7 (paperback)
ISBN: 978-1-7352279-0-0 (ebook)

For bulk sales or other information contact:

Crystal Bentley
E-mail: Crystal@SunAndStork.com
www.SunAndStork.com

My Way Too Long Dedication Page…

This book is dedicated to the wind beneath my wings, my Mom; Helen Furcron, my mother-in-law; Ina Bentley, my husband and graphic designer extrordinaire; Edward, our daughters; Lauren, Chelsea and Kaitlyn, my little Kahuna; Madison, my sisters, brothers, future son-in-laws, brother-in-laws, nieces, nephews and my tribe of friends, relatives and every student I've taught.

I also have to add the unexpected person who forced me to move forward and complete this book, Lynn S. You never know who your supporters are going to truly be in life – in this case – Lynn, the lunch monitor at my school kept me in line just like she kept the children (and we needed it)! Gosh, I love that lady! Thank you for holding me accountable! Now you've got to help me with the next one Lynn – let's eat cafeteria food and do this!

SUN WAS IN DISBELIEF!

"THIS CAN'T BE TRUE. HOW COULD HUMANS HAVE FORGOTTEN? HOW COULD THEY HAVE A CONVERSATION ABOUT THEIR COVERING WITHOUT MENTIONING MY GIFT? AFTER ALL, THEY COULDN'T HAVE FLOURISHED IN THEIR ENVIRONMENT ON EARTH WITHOUT IT! HOW DID OUR STORY BECOME LOST?"

You may be wondering why Sun was so upset and I don't blame you. Let me share what led Sun to this moment.

A few months ago, Sun was having a splendid conversation with Stork, until she shared distressing news. Stork overheard humans discussing their beautiful array of skin colors, but they appeared not to know how it came to be!!!!

Sun knew something had to be done, so he sent this story back to Earth with Stork! Do you know why humans come in so many magnificent colors? Do you know the story of Stork and Sun? If not, you simply must read this story and the record will be set straight!

I KNOW YOU WILL DELIGHT IN THE STORY OF SUN AND STORK.

A long time ago when the world was still new, Sun noticed a familiar sight in the distance. It was his oldest and dearest friend, Stork.

Stork and Sun had been friends for as long as he could remember — so long ago in fact, Sun couldn't remember how or when they met *(which isn't really surprising since both Sun and Stork are very, very, very old!)*

However, Sun certainly could remember all the fun and adventure he and Stork used to share when they were young. They had so much fun gliding through the Milky Way and exploring the galaxy!

As Sun watched his old friend approaching, he felt excitement in his stomach *(or as close to a stomach as a sun can have)*. You see, Sun always enjoyed when Stork stopped by to chat. Stork's visits were always an adventure. Stork always had fascinating deliveries! Sun chuckled to himself, as he recalled Stork trying to balance a pair of blue whales destined for the Pacific Ocean.

His thoughts then shifted to the time Stork had to deliver a pair of wattle cup caterpillars to Australia, before they turned into butterflies! Stork flew as fast as light!!

As Stork flew closer, Sun wondered how she was able to withstand the intensity of his beams. You see, Sun is *very, very, very* large and *very, very, very* hot! Sun started wondering if Stork was magical! Fortunately, whatever Stork carried in her silk parcel was protected from Sun's life nourishing, but extreme heat as well!

Stork hovered close to Sun with a big grin. She knew Sun was anxiously awaiting her newest delivery. Since Stork liked to playfully tease Sun, she delayed any talk about the delivery. She decided to talk to Sun about the galaxy of all things!!! Sun knew everything there was to know about the galaxy! After all, he watched fiery meteoroids, streaking comets, brilliant stars, vast planets and even swirling nebula all day and night! Since Sun knew Stork was teasing, he went along with Stork's joking!

After a while, Sun couldn't wait any longer and exclaimed "Stork! Okay! You win! What's in the bundle this time? You have such a look of pride! It's GOT TO BE SPECIAL!!!" Sun couldn't wait for an answer, so he began to guess, "Is it a pair of triceratops?"
Upon further thought, Sun started to mutter to himself, "No....It can't be any kind of dinosaur. She hasn't delivered dinosaurs in ages."

Sun guessed again. "What about a pair of fluffy, rainbow colored, cotton-tailed rabbits with large, buck teeth?" They both giggled at the thought! Stork smiled with pride as she knew Sun would never guess the mystery moving ever so slightly in her trusty, silken cloth. Stork spoke mysteriously, "You have never met creatures like these." Sun was curious indeed!
He begged, "Please let me see them Stork!"

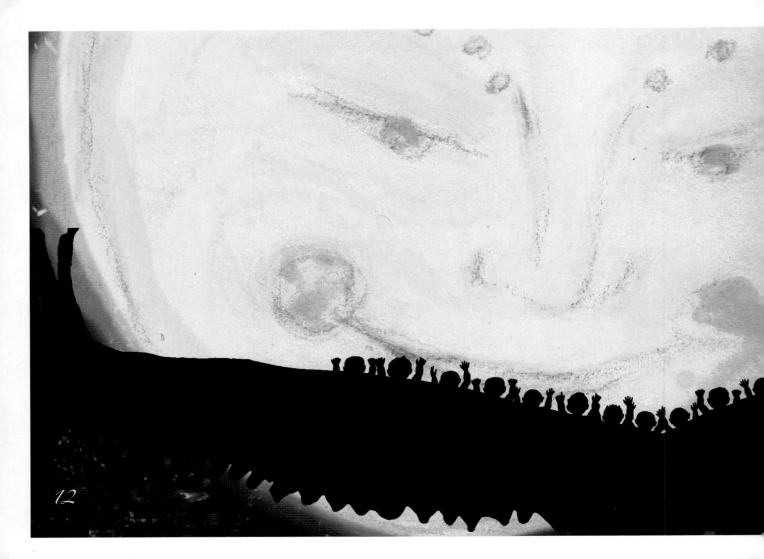

Stork decided she had teased Sun enough. Besides, she had to deliver her parcel to Earth. Stork gently maneuvered the pink satchel on her back and revealed 14 enchanting creatures. Sun gasped!!!!! He had never seen a delivery such as this. Sun gushed, "I think they are the cutest creatures I've ever seen!" The sounds they made were soothing and melodic, as they cooed and moved their arms and legs. Sun asked, "They are the perfect….ummmm….Stork…..what are they?"

Stork answered in a proud tone. "They are humans." Stork could tell Sun was pleased with the sight of the humans. Sun shone brighter than Stork could ever recall. In fact, Sun was so bright that Stork could no longer see his eyes, nose, or mouth, which really isn't very shocking since he is *very, very, very* bright!

After Sun stopped gazing at the adorable humans, he looked at Stork and asked softly, "Where are you delivering them?"

Stork replied "I am delivering a pair of infants to areas which will one day be known as the seven continents of Earth."

"Infants? I thought you said they were humans," Sun said curiously?

"Oh yes", Stork declared! "They are humans. However, when they are this young, we call them babies or infants."

"Ohhhhh! Infants," Sun said proudly.

Stork continued,
"I will be delivering a pair to an area which will one day be called

Africa...

"You know these areas well", Stork cheerfully shared as she flew closer to her friend. Sun agreed, "Yes, I know Earth very well and I'm concerned for these infants. Try as I might, I cannot give the same amount of my rays to every region on Earth! The amount of sun that reaches each area is quite different. Stork knew Sun was *very, very, very* concerned! Whenever Sun was perplexed or confused, his rays would begin to curve and look like question marks! Also, he emitted large patches of colors! Secretly, Stork loved when this happened since the tranquil blue reminded her of the cool, refreshing water on Earth.

Although Stork enjoyed the display of color, she wanted to help her friend. Stork asked caringly, "Why does the amount of sun you give to each region trouble you when it comes to the infants?"

Sun explained, "Almost all creatures on Earth need my rays to survive, and I know these infants will need my help." Stork admitted she still did not understand Sun's concern.

Sun explained "You are taking the infants to Earth, a planet with very different climates. Some infants will get so much sun that their covering will need protection from my intense rays, while others will go to places that will not get much sunshine. Some areas even go months without sun! The covering of those infants will need a way to easily take in the power of my rays! I didn't worry about the coverings of the other creatures you have taken to Earth. They have had something special about their covering to help with their climate! I am concerned because these infants do not. All of their covering is the same!"

'You're right", Stork happily exclaimed! "For instance, when I delivered hippopotamuses to Africa, a region where you shine intensely, the hippos were able to protect their skin by producing red sweat with sunscreen!

When I delivered zebra fish to South Asia, another region where your rays are very strong, the zebra fish were able to produce their own sunscreen as well.

I also recall the polar bears I flew to the Artic, a freezing cold region which does not receive the full power of your rays, were very prepared too! The polar bears' fur looked white, but was transparent to help your rays get through. Also, their black skin helped absorb your rays to heat their body!

Now, Stork was concerned. She looked down into the pink parcel and couldn't help but smile at the cooing infants. Stork took a closer look at their smooth skin and softly said "I understand your concern with their covering Sun, which is called skin. The infants need the power in your rays to survive. They need to get the right amount of sun for the climate. How can you help?"

Sun beamed and proudly said, "I can help their skin, Stork!" Stork was *very, very, very* confused! Sun smiled and said, "Don't worry! Just watch!"

In an instant, Sun gave a special kiss to each infant. They started to glow....then.... Stork was amazed at what happened next!

"Sun! Look at the infants! Their skin is no longer the same!"

The infants are now beautiful colors—colors I've seen in nature on Earth. The colors remind me of the bronze leaves of the maple tree in fall, the blush of an apricot, the light pink of tropical beach sand, the array of tones in a quartz stone, the rich hues of the chestnut, the glow of the desert sand, and the creaminess of a pale rose.

Sun was so proud and said, "Yes, Stork, I have given a special kiss to each baby so each will have my special protection in their skin. From the coldest regions that scarcely get sun, to the areas where I shine most intense. Each child's skin will be able to get the nourishment they need from me."

Both Sun and Stork were delighted and proud! They knew the Sun's kiss would help the infants not only survive, but thrive!

Stork had never been prouder of her friend, Sun. The infants cooed even louder, as if to thank Sun. As Sun watched Stork fly off into the distance, he was overcome with a sense of warmth. He gave the infants the best gift possible. Sun hoped the children of Earth would always look at each other and remember the gift he gave to them and always wear it with love and pride wherever they may go.

The End

By the way, Stork decided not to deliver the infants to Antarctica.
It was too cold!
Instead, she delivered those two infants to...oh, no!!!!

Stork has decided to tease you! Where do you think she delivered them?

Made in the USA
Columbia, SC
24 July 2020